ALL ABOUT WINTER

# Christmas

WITHDRAWN

by Martha E. H. Rustad

Consulting Editor: Gail Saunders-Smith, PhD

Mankato, Minnesota

Pebble Plus is published by Capstone Press,
151 Good Counsel Drive, P.O. Box 669, Mankato, Minnesota 56002.
www.capstonepress.com

1 2 3 4 5 6 13 12 11 10 09 08

*Library of Congress Cataloging-in-Publication Data*
Rustad, Martha E. H. (Martha Elizabeth Hillman), 1975–
    Christmas / by Martha E. H. Rustad.
    p. cm. — (Pebble plus. All about winter)
    Includes bibliographical references and index.
    Summary: "Simple text and photographs present the winter holiday, Christmas" — Provided by publisher.
    ISBN-13: 978-1-4296-2203-5 (hardcover)
    ISBN-10: 1-4296-2203-2 (hardcover)
    1. Christmas — Juvenile literature. I. Title. II. Series.
GT4985.5R87 2009b
394.2663 — dc22                                        2008003334

**Editorial Credits**
Sarah L. Schuette, editor; Veronica Bianchini, designer; Marcy Morin, photo shoot scheduler

**Photo Credits**
Capstone Press, 7
Capstone Press/Karon Dubke, all (except pg. 7)

## Note to Parents and Teachers

The All about Winter set supports national science standards related to changes during
the seasons. This book describes and illustrates the winter holiday, Christmas. The
images support early readers in understanding the text. The repetition of words and
phrases helps early readers learn new words. This book also introduces early readers
to subject-specific vocabulary words, which are defined in the Glossary section. Early
readers may need assistance to read some words and to use the Table of Contents,
Glossary, Read More, Internet Sites, and Index sections of the book.

# Table of Contents

# Christmas Is Coming!

Christmas Day is on
December 25.
Christians celebrate
the birth of Jesus Christ
on this holiday.

Jesus lived more than
2,000 years ago.
Jesus taught people to be
kind and loving to others.

# Getting Ready

We get ready

for Christmas in December.

We put up a tree.

We decorate it with lights

and ornaments.

We shop for presents.
We wrap them and set them
under the Christmas tree.

# Family Traditions

Grandma Gerry

bakes Christmas cookies.

She decorates them

with frosting and candy.

Angela's family
goes to church.
They pray
and sing songs.

Cord eats with his family.
They have carrots, ham,
and mashed potatoes.

# Santa

Santa is a symbol
of the Christmas spirit.
He reminds people to be
giving all year long.

19

We leave milk
and cookies for Santa
on Christmas Eve.
Merry Christmas!

# Glossary

**celebrate** — to do something fun on a special occasion or to mark a major event

**decorate** — to add items to something to make it prettier; people decorate trees and their homes to celebrate Christmas.

**holiday** — a festival or holy time; people usually take time off work, school, or regular activities during holidays.

**Jesus Christ** — the man Christians worship as the son of God

**ornament** — a small object used as a decoration

**symbol** — an object or person that reminds people of something else

# Read More

Houghton, Gillian. *Christmas = Navidad.* My Library of Holidays. New York: PowerKids Press, 2004.

Rustad, Martha E. H. *Christmas in Many Cultures.* Around the World. Mankato, Minn.: Capstone Press, 2009.

# Internet Sites

FactHound offers a safe, fun way to find Internet sites related to this book. All of the sites on FactHound have been researched by our staff.

Here's how:

1. Visit *www.facthound.com*

2. Choose your grade level.

3. Type in this book ID **1429622032** for age-appropriate sites. You may also browse subjects by clicking on letters, or by clicking on pictures and words.

4. Click on the **Fetch It** button.

**FactHound will fetch the best sites for you!**

# Index

Word Count: 129
Grade: 1
Early-Intervention Level: 14